The Very Now Poems

Jane Michelson Vuglar

Copyright © 2024 Jane Michelson Vuglar

The moral right of the author has been asserted.

Cover artwork copyright © Rowan Vuglar
Cover photography copyright © Geir Engene

Apart from any fair dealing for the purposes of research or private study, or criticism or review, as permitted under the Copyright, Designs and Patents Act 1988, this publication may only be reproduced, stored or transmitted, in any form or by any means, with the prior permission in writing of the publishers, or in the case of reprographic reproduction in accordance with the terms of licences issued by the Copyright Licensing Agency. Enquiries concerning reproduction outside those terms should be sent to the publishers.

Troubador Publishing Ltd
Unit E2 Airfield Business Park,
Harrison Road, Market Harborough,
Leicestershire. LE16 7UL
Tel: 0116 2792299
Email: books@troubador.co.uk
Web: www.troubador.co.uk

ISBN 978 1 80514 141 9

British Library Cataloguing in Publication Data.
A catalogue record for this book is available from the British Library.

Typeset in 10pt Minion Pro by Troubador Publishing Ltd, Leicester, UK

Acknowledgements

There are many who have helped me produce *The Very Now Poems*: thank you, all of you, for your patience and your time. Especial thanks to those at Troubador Publishing.

Rowan Vuglar, a dedicated artist who gave me the confidence to work solidly on the poems, prompting the first collection, *Walking the River*. For his loving support, critical feedback, his cooking – broccoli, carrots & kindness; for reproducing some of his paintings as illustrations.

Joshua Vuglar For his unfailing support, his love, his techie hints, his phone videos of new poems at the dinner table; my first website; his culinary delights and conversation.

Beckie Smith For her patience and support; her insight into 21st century technology; the new ideas she has brought us; her courage and companionship.

My beloved mother, Imi, for all that she did out of love for me, from encouraging my first wave of poetry/prose to acting, albeit briefly, as roadie and co-performer; our beloved books.

My father, who taught me self-reliance, and that life is about weathering change. For the smile in his eyes.

Brenda and Simon Michelson, for their kind support and thoughtfulness.

Sharon Goldstein, my cousin, for always being there; for her generosity of spirit; her faith in me that prompted the second wave of my work, after a long absence.

Dr. Andrew Goldstein Rabbi Emeritus author of Judith's Diaries, for encouragement and helpful advice, his understanding and love of poetry.

Tammy Goldstein Graphic Designer for her fine work on *Walking the River* (see above) and **Rabbi Aaron Goldstein**, for their kindly support and inspiration.

Ruth Colin for her help in a time of darkness and **Richard Colin**, our go-to-person in times of distress (technical and other) who enabled my work through his gift of time and expertise.

To all of my family and friends (especially Joseph). Their feedback/keen-eyed criticism, when deluged with various versions of poems, has kept me balancing on my poetic toes.

Jenny Vuglar, Caroline Williamson, Rosemary Norman and **Daphne Rock**, fellow poets of the Foxhall Women's Writers' Group for their critical support with my first wave poems & prose.

Chantal Coady, Rococo Chocolates and Chocolate Detective for The Comfort of Chocolate.

All the family and friends who have shared their homes with us, providing a much needed respite and space to create, far from the inner clutter of home and city.

Jennifer Knight and **Cecily Solomons**, for being there.

My loving family for clubbing together to support this publishing venture. Grateful thanks to Rowan, Josh & Beckie; Auntie Davene & Uncle Lawrence Bader (another fine painter); my cousins: Graham & Avril, Sharon & Andrew, Jennie, Alison and Marvin; Aaron & Tammy, Ruth and Richard; the great nephew, Joseph and great nieces: Jemima, Liora & Shaya; the "ganze mishpocha" family: Gilda & Bernard, Penny & Paul.

The NHS (Mawbey group practice/Guy's/St Thomas'/King's College Hospitals) for their dedicated care.

Special thanks to The Needlecraft Shop, Beccles for inspiring Emporium, and for permission to use the accompanying photograph.

Thanks also, to Bramleys Tea Rooms, St Florence, Wales – for that wondrous Sunday Lunch.

And finally, Sharon Goldstein and the family for so many excellent Puddings!

Contents

Disclosure	1
Frog in Appley Bridge	2
Acacia at Kew	3
The Botanical Garden	4
Lament for Westminster Adult Education Service	6
Austerity	7
No Time to Close Your Eyes	8
Divorced Child	9
Dark Matter	10
Imprint	12
The Room of my Dreams	13
To Sarah	14
Mavis	15
Slipper Socks	16
Material Pleasures	19
Deep Waters	20
Hospital Visit 1990	22
Moby Jane	23
Summer Bright	24
Growing Pains	25
Man up a Ladder	26
So Many	28
3 a.m.	29
Freeze	30

6am	32
Anything Human	33
Lockdown Lament	34
On the Way Back	36
The Visitor	38
Cat and Mouse	40
What of Love	41
Sunday Lunch	42
Woolly Thinking	43
Puddings	44
Rising	45
Emporium	46
All Along	48
Flaming London	49
Days	50
Bits of Me	51
Gull and Chips	52
The Comfort of Chocolate	54
Pigeon Pecked	55
Parallel	56
Ratty	58
Manorbier	60
Sunburn	62
Patient Waiting	63
Motorbike	64
The Aquadrome	65
Another Year	67

Disclosure

I have stepped out of my closet, that warm dark place
where moths feast hungrily on impartial wool,
leave empty holes in place of yarn;
out of my cramped wardrobe, bustled with angular
hangars, their thin wire-crooked elbows.

Nowadays, I blare out my words on street corners
(or the social media equivalent) to all-comers.
Ghost me as you will, the poems will fly,
humming quietly to themselves through cyberspace.

Recite them on the telephone, the cherished landline
to which I cling all my days, mourning only those kinked
coils of wire, the alphabet dial, the crossed lines where
random callers met in brief exchange of strange civility.

I breeze my poems, if you linger long enough.
Would you care to hear one?
It's a bit ancient mariner who stoppeth one, two, three,
but hey, no mothballs on me, sweet cedar or rank chemical
lurking in forgotten pockets.

And if their eyes glaze like iced doughnuts, their smiles ice
into weary politeness, it is all one with me: for at my back
times' winged chariot is wish-swishing over limitless seas.
Eternity is calling; Dover Beach is rustling its waves
over the shingle and Coleridge is spinning his long yarn.

Frog in Appley Bridge

Frog sits in tiny pond,
still as still, head protruding
through speckled duckweed;
watching with fierce attention
summer flies skimming by,
near but not near enough.

Purple loosestrife sways
in the breeze, aslant
like teenagers propping bikes.

Bees buzzing, birds crooning.
A petal drifts onto the frog's eye;
its encrusted neck lifts, sinks
beneath the leaf-green mat.

An incautious movement; a second frog,
a raised mound of leaf water
below the surface, its skin
all over duckweed.

Crocosmia wavers its fiery flowers,
fallen petals drift flame on water;
submerged, liquid green frogs
lie in wait, tongues curled
in readiness to snap up
tiny gems of skittering flies.

Acacia at Kew

The Acacia Horrida is no soft plant
to garnish a window sill.

The Horrida, as you'd expect,
specialises in thorns, not flowers:
rigid pairs of whitish thorns
like mutant cat whiskers.

It is armed to fight off predators
in the hungry places of East Africa,
India, Australia. Its roots intransigent,
blindly it seeks out the deep down water.

Sleeping Beauty could have slept on
in peace, guarded by an acacia horrida
prickled hedge; yet its flowers are soft
inflorescence sun gold pompoms.

Brisk gardeners measure humidity,
temperatures raised to the tropics:
it is a long way from home.
There are glass walls to guard it,
keep it safe. No bees harvest it for honey.

Outside, it is raining again.
Daffodils clump in the wet grass,
wind whistles through the trees.
Aeroplanes travel low overhead
from this place to that, and back again.

The Botanical Garden

Out of the crevices of warm stone,
by the flowered pathways,
lizards slip across the stacked rocks
with barely a whisper,
their sinuous bodies green waves
fluttering over step and earth.

One settles amiably on a high stone ledge,
complacent in the warm sun.
Its eyes blink its surroundings,
aware of every thrill of vibration,
every human tread
along the Mediterranean pathway.

A pair of brown lizards sweep
companionably together across cracked earth.
Rain is due; the ground freshens.
A grove of olive trees look to the sky,
where rain clouds hover until the wind shifts.

The wild wall lizards lie and wait
for the empty peace of evening;
visitors to cease their trample;
the ponderous bipeds to head home
with their dogs and umbrellas.

The rain is long gone.
A moon-lit night, the rustle of dry leaves;
sleeping lizards, green and brown,
dream of insect breakfasts, spider luncheons,
cricket teas, bathed in the warmest of sunshine.

Lament for Westminster Adult Education Service

formerly part of the Inner London Education Services,
the I.L.E.A. abolished in 1990

Adult Ed is on the wane:
our grants are slashed. It is in vain
we counter with our worthy aims
And
there's nowhere to store the timpani.

Now our usual classes come
priced at an astronomic sum:
would-be students are struck dumb
And
there's nowhere to store the timpani.

Next year's programme has unrolled;
successful classes set to fold.
This world is chillier than of old-
And
nowhere to store the timpani.

So this is then a sad lament
for the good old days, when students went
in happy teeming hordes, intent
on fun and learning.

Not *just* "Vocational", not *just* "Leisure":
friendship, work, deep-seated pleasure,
warmth, companionship unmeasured-
And
always, there was room for the timpani!

Austerity

Debts bought and sold, packaged so fine,
shuffled, repackaged, sold on:
a veritable goldmine.

It was Pass the Parcel till the music stopped.
The cupboard was bare:
people had to go live in a shoe; or a shoebox.
But shoeboxes lack basic amenities.

Money had to be found.
The banks squealed and squealed:
poor little piggies -no roast beef,
their curly tails drooped as they ran all the way home.

So the king and the queen and their chancellor
came up with a Cunning Plan:
everyone could pay, this was called Austerity.
Wages were frozen; benefits cut,
except for the king, the queen, the chancellor,
the lords and ladies, who rode snow white steeds.

Winter filled the land; the people shivered:
they warmed their hands by candle light;
Libraries closed but no books burnt for warmth.
Refuges shut their doors. The homeless
looked for shoes, which didn't pinch;
the hungry dined from food banks;
the old remembered the war.
Life was no fairy tale.

No Time to Close Your Eyes

This is no time to close your eyes
to politicians' self-aggrandising lies.
Watch them rebrand facts as fiction:
oh, that privileged public school diction.

Cui bono? Who gets the billions?
A clue: not us nor the millionaires' minions.
Zero contracts yield vast profit;
shareholders don't share- so, what of it?

Austerity is the price we paid
for bankers gambling, unafraid;
debts passed on to you and me.
Wave farewell to society.

Remember Barnard Castle? Test your eyes,
who can spot self-serving lies?
Flat refurbishment? Cheap at the price.
We all want the new home to look nice.

In this, the age of the pandemic,
corporate looting is systemic.
Huge profits don't come from volunteers:
they're amassed by privateers.

Hold down your pay as inflation rockets high.
All in it together? It's a barefaced lie.

Divorced Child

I waited all that autumn
for my father to gallop over,
sling us cheerfully across his saddle
and ride us home to forgiveness.

Waiting stolidly all winter:
it was just a matter of time.
Spring, summer shredded past
as we settled into a regular routine.

The call would come,
a long-delayed telegram arrive;
hooves pounding the gravel drive,
to the amazement of the neighbours.

Impermanence flowed in my blood.
One day I simply forgot
what we waited for.

It was enough that we waited,
mother and I, roped together
like abandoned hostages.

I've sworn to wait for his coming,
no matter how long.
But I wish he'd hurry.
Mother and I can't wait for ever.

Dark Matter
for Joseph

Thick tufts of dark matter
hide in plain sight:
non baryonic, emit no light.
Somewhat ironic, existence inferred,
in the beginning was the word.

2.41 x 10 to the minus twenty-seven;
earth we know, but what of Heaven?
We are such very small fry:
in our muddy puddles, the sun-lit sky.

All quarks are fermions,
with a half spin.
How can we tell
What world we are in?

Up quark, down quark, strange quark, charm,
bottom quark, antiquark: red, green, blue.
We stumble through a night-time forest
we thought we knew.

The fifth Greek element was Quintessence:
antimatter its very essence.
Dark matter weaves between the stars.
Perseverence is alive on Mars.

Imprint

In that cat-cradle time,
books came first:
all our old favourites
packed spine to spine
in dark crates.

We trailed our tea-chests
across England,
harried, on the move.

My parents' marriage ended
with the division
of their Companion Book Club collection.

Dad tacked off
with the Art of Coarse Sailing;
mum kept Kipling and Hobbes.

With me too, it's books first;
my life a tracery of print,
watermark and folio:
a world of clean unbroken spines.

The Room of my Dreams
To Alison Fell

The room of my dreams
when the other horse died
in an explosion of yellow rays:
it was that kind of day.

It rains in the North,
spattering the willow trees.
I can hardly breathe in
daddy's death.

Kind man driving:
there are some very kind men,
but always the echo behind.

Daddy shouting, grandpa dying,
it's turned us sight bright, fast-moving.
Astonishingly, the death of black and white.

The room of my dreams when the other horse died,
under arcs of red brick. My arms and hers
in an explosion of yellow rays.
It rains in the North.

I can hardly breathe in, sight bright, fast-moving,
the death of black and white.

Daddy shouting, grandpa dying.
Astonishingly, it's snowing.
The other horse died.

To Sarah

Curled up in the warm embrace of sleep,
I dreamt of you,
my sister, so far apart
so often out of sync;
listening out for one another,
as if we breathed the same air.

You were the cuckoo in my nest,
the feathered intruder;
whilst I, amid shards of shell,
lay on the cold pavement,
blinking in surprise.

Invited for a visit,
I gazed at your curious face
pushed past in a perambulator,
blue eyes smiling up at me
in amiable thought,
a gurgle of delight on your lips.

I held you in my arms,
so peaceful
close to my heart.
We are sisters.

Mavis

Her stomach, it was, banished us our beloved haunt
behind unlovely Digbeth bus station, its barren
reach of empty grass, blind lamp posts, tossed cans;
across gloomy sweep of tarmac, past shuttered shops,
to The Jug O' Punch, to The Holy Ground itself.

In the half-light, throaty men mouthed obscene jokes,
sang like angels. Irish laments keened a path through
the dense pall of smoke, where drunken men cried for
the Republic; crashed their tankards against stained tables.

Her stomach swelled fat as a balloon and more than air
was in it. Near home, the Sorrento Maternity, so they
murmured, took unmarried mothers with their shame.

She stood before the altar, before God Almighty,
beside the boyish groom, togged up in his best.
Her family patrolled the church in suits and hats;
listened hard-eyed for each word of the marriage vow.
Her stomach poked the pale lemon dress into a round dumpling.

An Irish fiddler played at the wedding.

Slipper Socks
for Beryl and Elise

2 oz ply wool (No.4 needles for lady's size)

Wool shops in the High St,
wooden shelves crammed:
layers of soft yarn, shade on shade,
palest of pinks swanning into deep crimsons,
primrose yellows into rich mustard gold.

Oz, the ounce, sixteen to the pound weight.
Women were all ladies. Gender fixed
like the sun, the moon and the stars,
from the first wet gasp of breath.
Mothers, aunts, grandparents knitting:
pastel blue bootees (boys) rose pink (girls).
Knitting for the yet-to-be-born, cream or daisy yellow.
So straightforward, no question. Like a knitting pattern.

Abbreviations k-knit. Tog.-together. p-purl
PSSO-pass slip-stitch over

You sat quietly knitting; it keeps my hands occupied,
you said,
twisting the yarn with a deft assurance.

INSTRUCTIONS
Cast on 29 stitches.

Looping each stitch onto the needle.
It is a beginning. They hang from the needle
like a warm promise.

1ˢᵗ row…k9: p 1: k9: p1: k9
2ⁿᵈ row…Knit all the row
Repeat these 2 rows 18 times.

27 twisted loops and 2 straight stitches
18 rows, 18 years in a serried row,
typing in a typing pool, retyping,
arthritic fingers pound metal keys;
work in triplicate with inky carbon. Clatter
echoing click and clack of your straight needles
knitting milk-white Aran jumpers and dark blue guernseys,
against the bitter winters of our childhood. And bootees.

Next row p 1: k 1: across row
Then k 1: p 1: across row
Repeat these two rows 6 times

Shabbat Friday with your sister; the house perfumed with
the warm smells of freshly fried fish, gefilte fish, gherkins.
2 ladies knitting, 2 sets of needles chattering together.
K tog. Sharing slipped stitches as sisters do.

Toe Decrease
1st row…Rib 7: slip 1: k 1 PSSO k 1: k 2 tog Rib 5: k 2 tog k 1:
sl.1: k 1: PSSO Rib 7
2nd row…Rib 7: p 3: Rib 5: p 3: Rib 7
3rd row…Rib 6: sl. 1: k 1: PSSO k 1: k 2 tog: Rib 3: k 2 tog:
k 1: sl. 1: k 1: PSSO. Rib 6
4th row…Rib 6: p 3: Rib 3: Rib 6:

Cut wool.

Her finger and thumbs slide through the soft woollen yarn.
The gramophone plays Vaughan Willliam's Pastoral Symphony.
She listens as her needles twist and turn; she has heard it many times.
It chimes with her own quiet air of abstraction. Evening falls. Again.

Material Pleasures

My mother bought
a dark leather three-piece
suite at the Sales.

It sat uneasily in the lounge,
despite earnest rearranging
by myself and a brace of aunts.

It lowered at the nest
of tables; gloomed Byronically
at the family photos.

On hot days the suite smelled
of long-dead cow.

Sadly my mother swapped it
for her sister's dralon set,
out of which she could lever herself to standing
in seconds.

The leather three-piece trundled
down the motor-way to Birmingham.

"A moment of mad folly," sighed mother,
but she hung on to the foot stool
for emergencies.

Deep Waters

Bubbeleh lives between chair and bed,
pleats and repleats the coverlet;
folds it as if it were a love letter,
a keepsake from the Great War.
That cherished letter he sent,
knee deep in mud and bones:
"Dear Katy, he wished me to write
in case. He died a soldier's death."

Few words she can utter now.
The broken connection severed the wellspring
of words, silenced her stories. Yet her eyes
still sometime hold that far off gleam.

From the Pale of Russia, with her infant sisters
over the vast sea-green waves,
as the nineteenth century ebbed and flowed
into the unsteady twentieth:
Pogroms, world wars, the Holocaust
and she the enemy alien.

Those who lived: the brave, the saved,
the downright lucky. Jews who thrived,
lived nervously joyful lives.
So few, when once so many.
My grandmother spoke Yiddish.

Lustrous long plaits, carefully arranged
to resemble the traditional wig, the sheitel,
she was her own woman.
Married the Jew who wrote her
of her friend Sam's death,
that morning in the autumn of the war.

Katy, Katya, Kit, my grandmother.
Weep, for the deep waters have taken you,
the sea-green waves, the swelling tide
that swept you here,
reclaimed you for their own.

My grandmother looks up,
sees us sitting there
with fresh barley water;
and her smile is piercing sweet.

Hospital Visit 1990

The nurse said, "You can see him now.
He's awake." My father ensconced
in his private hospital, humming with quiet.

I, his daughter, falter on the threshold
of an unwelcome intrusion.
Tap shyly on the closed door, unused
to visiting unannounced, unexpected.

The door is firmly shut on his blocked arteries.
Yesterday, they breached the heart wall,
attached a double bypass.

Years back, he traded his life and family
for the snowy glitter of virgin slopes:
it was the Sixties, the Age of Aquarius.

Snow turned to ice; winter melted;
he journeyed on, leaving the past behind
to fend for itself; sailed into calmer seas.

There are stitches lacing his chest:
the operation went well. He smiles up at me,
his daughter, awkward in this clean room.
Gallant in pyjamas, bleary with anaesthetic,
he gazes up at me, with amused recognition.

Moby Jane

Once my own woman
from the crown of my head
down to the tip of my toes,
I fell in love
with a New Zealander.

A man of quiet strength,
he corralled me
with a smile as urgent
as a whistle.

I had known others,
but he was the one
well met at midnight
in the unlit kitchen,
rummaging the fridge.

Together, to our surprise,
we begat.
My sylph-like figure
became blubber; my gait
slowed to a wistful wobble.

I am become the great white whale
cruising the depths,
with an eye glazed open
for net curtains and crochet hooks.

Summer Bright

The children are knocking at the door.
Is he in? Can he come out to play?
Urgent faces looking up at us,
the big ones, the decision-makers.

Nearly nine, but full summer;
the streets are light, the gardens beckon.
Children are calling, calling in the street.
There's a picnic in progress on the cleared asphalt;
Two Swings garden, they sit on the grassy mound,
discuss great matters.

It's late; ours has eaten, was quietly reading.
This is summer and the children are calling
at each separate door, Can he come out now?
Flocking together on the warm pavements,
Hide and Seek, chasing each other down twisty paths.

The old warnings sing out.
It's a bit late. Stay together. Be back by…
They are gone, a flight of starlings, their shrill cries
swoop in and out of adventure until nightfall.

Parents stand, calling their children home:
their names ring out, echo in the falling dusk.
Have you seen? Are they at yours? Who were they with?
Knocking at each separate door, gathering them up
one by one, hauling them home. Bedtime, curled up in pjs:
they are no longer together, but they have all come home.

Growing Pains

Soft as butter, these children
at ten and fourteen,
their features still warm wax
around growing bone.

When anger or injustice strike,
they recoil,
whip back like a bank of snakes,
tongues alive with venom.

Then remorseful, offer up titbits
to placate,
win back a goodnight kiss, a smile,
with an easy gesture.

Hug them tight
before the gremlins get them,
warp them into sadness.
It is hard to be young.

Hug them tight
before their trustfulness yields:
there is still time
always
to feather their existence.

Man up a Ladder

When I see a man in white overalls,
his face marked with smears of paint and plaster,
my heart stops for a beat: so like, yet unlike him.

When first we met, you painted pictures, cherry blossom
on cerulean blue, tulips chattering
in a flower bed, against a wash of colour.

Then decade after decade you trudged up scaffolding,
balanced on ladders high and low, sandpaper and brush in hand;
your mission: to restore whole buildings to immaculate beauty,
return them to innocence.

Your down-a-heel studios, the long crumbling corridors,
room after room splashed with colour,
the buzz of saws, the bright splutter of an arc weld,
the fierce concentration of brush and chisel,
the lathe and the dancers.

Long gone that labyrinthine palace of art; gone its honey bee hives,
its rambling gardens, the plaster herons on the roof,
the outdoor easels, the trees.

In your solitary work stained overalls, you chipped away
at flakes of drifting plaster,
filled in gaps in the fabric of time.
My heart still misses a beat when I see a workman,
or a car crowned with ladders.

A quiet man, my second soul; white overalls smeared with pigment,
sunshine, trees and crescent moons on canvas and on paper,
paints the universe whole.

So Many

So many children sat here learning;
gradual gleaning, forward leaning
wrapped in seashell soft sand lying,
from the ebb tide soon returning
wind and salt waves brave defying.

All these children, once here sat
scuffling their feet on the woolly mat;
braced for change, pencils ready;
set fair for storm and sea rise eddy:
their feet now dry as they sail by,
their quiet gaze so steady.

3 a.m.

Wide awake. Bedclothes rumpled.
Can't sleep; brain all crumpled,
bedding an untidy heap.

That last dream left you shivery cold,
some ridiculous lonely absence.
They just were away, but oh so near:
delayed, that's all, but you felt such fear.
Woke up and found you were old.

Impossible to go back to sleep-
the loss, the fears, all too deep.
Lie there drained; an empty glass.
It's 3 a.m. this night will pass.

All over the city, all over the land,
people stare at the miserable clock.
Its hands move slower than holiday gridlock.
Will snatch some sleep, drowsed in a chair:
catnaps, 40 winks, a temporary affair.

Come the new day, the hours stroll past
loose-limbed, youthful, life's a blast!
Farewell those 3a.m. long stretches,
us sleepless, heavy eyed insomniac wretches.
The sun is risen, we'll brew some tea,
savour the new day stealthily.

Freeze

For Penny K

I am here but caught,
like a small gecko in a piece of peach amber.
Now and then, stopped entirely.

Yet I have not left.

Time slows, jumps in starts
as the signal drops out;
swims back through the thickening air.

I am still here

despite awkward stumble
where once I danced,
my hesitant tread does not lack grace.

Brain muddles ups and alongs:
I live inside an Escher painting;
my life does not lack drama.

Eyes and brain play tricks
but it has always been so,
conjuring our world out of slivers of perception.

Through the haze of tiredness,
I am seeing with open eyes.

Are you still seeing me?
I have not left.

Yes, there are cracks in the plaster
of my existence,
fault lines that sadden;
but the walls still stand:
the creamy ceiling stretches over my head,
like acres of warm snow.

6am

When the first light knocks plaintive at the door;
when the black of night rolls back its rug,
the moon shifts to day mode,
pale, like cheesecake.

Kettle mists rise with the first tea.
Are you awake now, this moment,
whispering into the kitchen on soft shoes;
ruminating on life turned quicksilver
in a splash of time?

Memories accrete
like burrs hooked onto a duffel coat;
autumn conkers hang vinegar brown on ropes of string;
forget-me-nots, glimmer blue with promise.

All these hours, all these days
hurtling past, halt at 6am for a breath of air
lit by the dawn sun
blinking the new day into existence.

Anything Human
A pandemic poem

There can exist a risk to anything human:
in standing too close, a reckless touch,
holding hands or more than hands.

We are under siege: fear frames our fragile existence.
Statistics stand like a beacon, warning the horizon:
Stay clear. Keep your distance.

We have been islands of sorrow, lonely and alone,
cut off from loved ones until their death day.

When you were young, you asked to take a gift
to a dying great-aunt. It's like a birthday, you argued,
but we took no gift. Perhaps we should have.

Now, the single gift is a visit in person, gowned and masked:
like the last rites of a Catholic priest, we are become
the Angel of Death. Distanced from touch,
from comfort transcends screen and glove,
what have we become?

The pandemic young learnt nearness spells danger. In the loop
of time as yet unravelled, will they flinch from those outside
their bubble existence, seek safety in cool solitude?

Let this world grow larger when all is done,
twirl soft like soap bubbles, a mad rainbow iridescence.

May they break from the spider web of fear, find touch more
precious than rubies, be foolish in love. Be human kind.

Lockdown Lament

You wake up slow,
feel like crap.
Getting out of bed,
can't handle that.   Sad face, sad face emoji.

Put on some clothes?
Forget it.
Did it a few times.
Regret it.   Upside-down-smiley-face emoji.

Lurking on my phone
in teddy pjs.
That's about it
most days.   Phone-in-hand emoji.

Messaging friends,
say I'm ok;
I'm really not.
I'm down today.   Fake-smiley-face emoji.

Lunchtime- open tin of beans.
Spoon out of tin.
Drink milk.
Must empty bin.   Won't emoji.

Mess about on phone,
watch a work-out.
On my own.
Give friend a shout.　　Calling-out emoji.

Time for tea.
Should really wash
but who gives a toss?
Not me.　　　　　　Can't-be-arsed emoji.

Honest truth,
live or die-
need hugs.
Not going to cry.　　Crying-face emoji.

On the Way Back
For Jennifer

After the ceremony, discreet silence.
music played as she slid away, unwilling,
through fierce funeral flames to eternity.

Not ready; thinking she had more time.
Always more time to fill: too much; then
not enough. Death took her by surprise;
laid her softly in a field of flowers.

Silent, we drove away; no lingering allowed
this fearful year; down a byway fringed with
forest. Clambered out for the necessary visit.

Hitched up my clothes in a leafy hollow
when a deer, eyes white with startlement,
its legs bunched in fright, so near, so very close
its breath puffed past like steam;
a second deer pounded after, brown fur gleaming.
In the afternoon sun, its eyes shone like water.

There had been tears for that pale thin woman:
daughter, widow, cousin, lifelong friend.
One day I would cease to grieve.

Today there was the comfort of deer, trotting
with a wild abandon that sang of life resurgent.

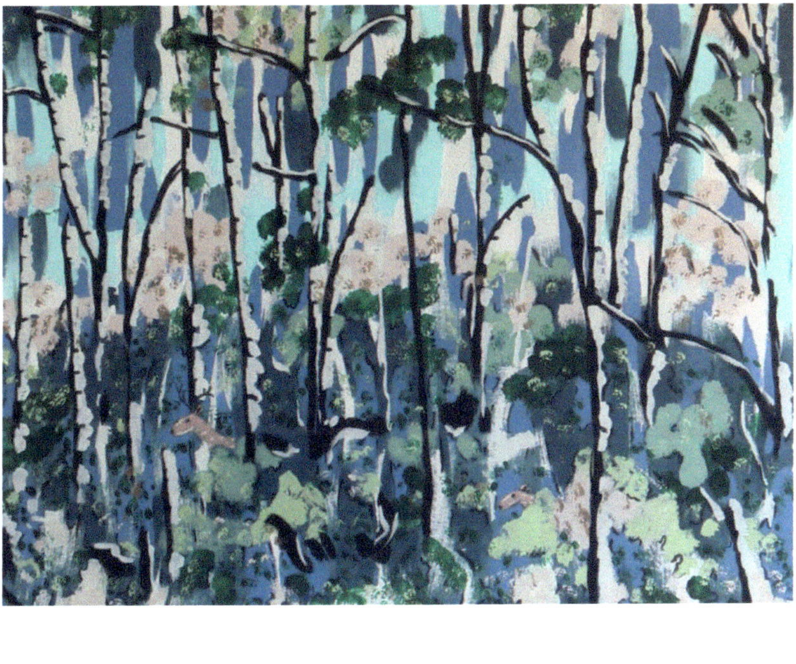

The Visitor
A true story

Part one: arrival

There is a big brown paper bag
inside a brown cardboard box
on the must-sort-sometime trolley,
in my everything room
where I eat, sleep, write with distraction.

Distracted now by a persistent rustle,
followed by a crumply clawing sound,
penetrates the forest of the room:
it is coming from the brown paper bag
inside the stiff brown cardboard box,
on the must-sort-sometime trolley.

Regret banishing elderly cat from the room
after unfortunate elderly episodes.
Brown bag twitches on the really-wish-I'd-sorted trolley.
Mice? Bubonic rat? Approaching with caution, when

Whoosh! A small bird rockets out of the bag
in the unfortunate brown box on the trolley;
flies up to the drooping curtain rail, clutches it
in wide-eyed fright; ricochets round the room
like a mad satellite, curtain rail to clothes rail,
to the literate bookcase; peers at its perch on
Jim Haynes' Thanks for Coming; flurries to the wardrobe,
toes fastened fast to my mother's gold-edged Pilgrim's Progress.

Part two: departure

Half the sash window open, half shut tight:
bird unable to deconstruct this,
flies at the topmost part; narrowly misses
glass pane concussion; reels back
to Harry Potter and the Prisoner of Askaban.

The old Dr Dolittle volumes drifting apart with age,
full of animal talk. "It's ok, bird," crooning sweetly.
"No need to panic. You can escape from this room."
Bird pays attention, listens and listens.

By the window, my arm between inside and out;
poke a rolled up newspaper through the airy gap,
again and once more: "This is the exit," I sing at the bird,
whistling and chirping. Bird watches, cogitates.

Then Whoosh! Small bird flies up to me,
trustingly hovers a moment by my anxious face,
wings beating like a stressed heart:
shoots out of the window in one brave arrow of flight.

I am alone again in my must-tidy room,
surrounded by the nowhere-else-to-put-it:
juggling balls, photo albums, tins of pilchards;
books, always books, and then the trolley.
Writing with distraction.

Cat and Mouse
an elegy

Remember the mice and the cat so old,
how they scampered through the house?
Poor old cat, his sight long gone
his hearing dim as dim,
wandered disconsolate the kitchen,
breathing the scent of mouse.

Behind the fridge, by cat tray corner,
upstairs behind the walls,
squeaky rustling little beasties
snuffled and ruffled in search of feasties.
Morning and evening, out they crept
while our ancient geriatric feline slept,
dreaming of long gone hunting days,
his triumphant caterwauls.

Mice now gone to where mice go;
barely a trace remains.
Cat shuffled off, all twitches and groans,
then no more aches and pains.
Cat flew up to feline heaven,
as he once shot up our stairs.
Eyes now bright and full of stars,
he hunts with the Lion and the Bear.

What of Love

Let us love those
who love regardless of binary him&her
sets of immaculate towels
biro blue, tulip pink;
whose love is unhedged by the fields
of separation: my partner, my companion,
my child, my cockapoo.

Those dry stone walls, each stone
angled into position, now soft with lichen:
love seeds itself on either side,
straddles the low walls,
flourishes beneath rock and stone.

Let us graze the sweet turf,
glance briefly up at the sunlit fells
as midday shadows pool;
there are alphabetical letters to pin down our love,
as if the effable were a mere trick of definition.

There is I and there is you:
as long as no-one is damaged
in their secret self,
we are together for always
as long as we are together,
you and I, our family, the cockapoo.

Sunday Lunch

Grandad is cooking for seventy.
5 roasts, all the slaughter of bird and beast
with nut roast for abstainers; followed by pavlova,
soft as sea foam, with a sprinkling of green kiwi, blush
strawberries, blueberries, the tart sweetness of red currants.

Daughters and granddaughters scurry between galley
and the tight cluster of tables: twos, some threes,
a brace of fours; ageing diners leaning forward to hear
above the echoing clatter and chatter.

Family waitresses hover solicitous, wings furled into aprons.
"Grandad and grandma back on Friday. Jet-lagged, they are.
We get to go to Center Parcs next month."

Sticks tap their way to the tables, shuffle into place, winter
anoraks shed with difficulty. Underneath, they're all spruced up:
necklace, rings, jacket, tie; grey hair nervous with elegance.

Twos and threes lean to one another; the fours sit back
in pairs, older and less old, straining to hear. Noise crescendos,
bounces off the shed walls, wooden slats studded with
scenic views, hung with draperies of large flat leaves.

The burble rises and falls like soap-blown bubbles; sinks and is
gone in the melee of old sound, as others lift into brief brightness;
hover above the clatter of eager cutlery. Voices whisper,
drone, moan, laugh and love. Outside the wind presses hard;
roses stretch their thorny branches into the icy breath of winter.

Woolly Thinking
for Iris

The sheep's gaze reproaches me,
that quiet sad look.
Oblivious of impending doom,
lambs are springing over the turf;
play chase with their friends,
just as my son did, limbs gawky like elbows.

My coat pockets are heavy and deep.

Vigorous old ladies stop us in the narrow street.
"May we look?" they ask politely. "Such fine work, isn't it?"
stroking his capacious jumper this way and that;
Iris's deft patchwork knit, a soft treasure
mapped in wool.

The ewe eyes me: her gaze penetrates my silent sympathy,
sees into the sophistry wrapped deep in my raw
coat pockets, leaking lightly inside the tidy parcel.

She turns away; I turn away
from the fields of grazing green,
distant fields dotted with white lambs.

One lamb is missing.

Puddings

There is happiness in puddings
of every description;
how much better we would feel
were they available on prescription.

Ice cream mounds of every flavour,
bitter-sweet chocolate, pale vanilla,
lemon drizzle cake, creamy plava,
lokshen pudding, desserts to crave for.

Soups and starters are all very well,
main courses have definite delight;
but a sugar-rich pud that does you no good
is the most magnificent sight.

Fruit has its place in a salad or dish,
Sweet melon, figs and grape;
lemon meringue and pumpkin pie,
Death by Chocolate cake.

So many magical puddings there are,
we save them for a special treat:
for holidays, special days, *not* everydays
or the sugar would have us beet.

Hurrah for rum baba, three cheers for baklava,
for puddings so splendidly sweet.

Rising

The temperature's rising,
it's hardly surprising.
The girl certainly could Can-Can.

The temperature's risen:
global warming derision.
Hey, anyone seen a fan-fan?

Long ago, dystopian visions.
Who wanted to know
petrol is no-go?
Not to mention sheep emissions.

Swirl those skirts, swing and rock;
tropical here, that sun don't stop.
Sun shines down; grass is straw;
bleached the earth; crops no more.

Sea levels rising. Not surprising,
low-lying islands lie below.
Swimming is de rigueur
while you still got the vigour
to paddle the seasonal flow.

Put on yr dancing shoes;
pirouette with flair,
Can-Can, swirl and spin.
Show us what you're made of.
This is where we came in.

Emporium

Here the fabric in wrapped rolls,
stacked and decked like human souls
waiting the call to heaven.

Here the buttons, shaped and sized:
pearl, coat brown, bright incised
boxed in rows of concentration.

Here the threads and here the wool:
all the shades, shyly colourful,
for the sharp-eyed needle.

Mist green, sand, milky cream hues,
Fierce fire- red, baby blues;
this windblown coast where
land greets the sinuous sea.

Refracted patterns weave daylight
into the patterns of the night
when angels descend.

This is the place where all things mend;
if it's straight, it still can bend
into the shape of light.

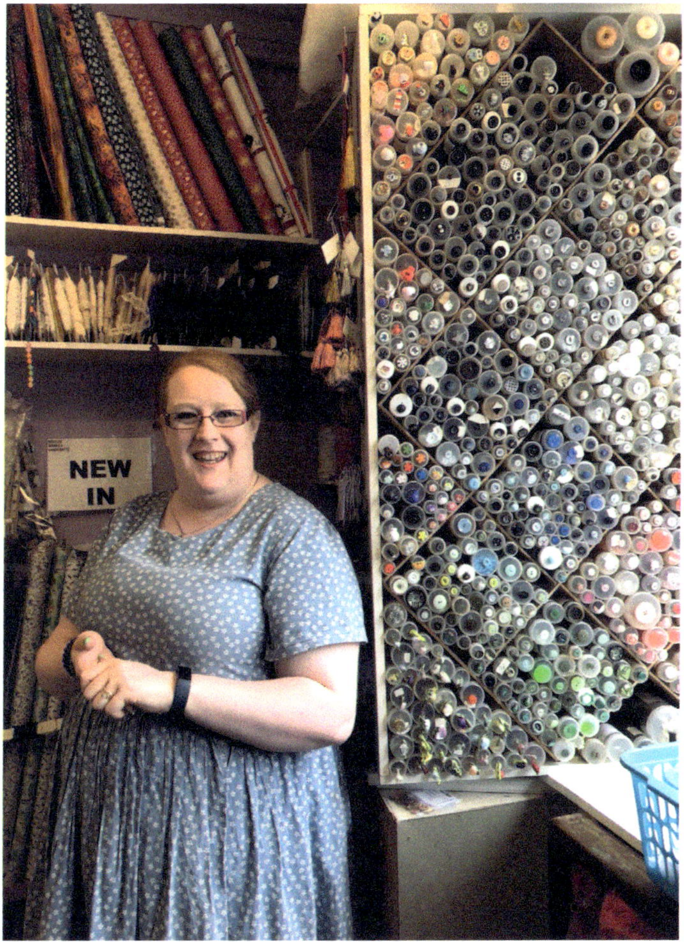
NEW
IN

All Along

All along the silver river,
thin moon squats the April sky,
soft pigment blue.

Low sun lights a thousand mirrors,
gleams blind glare in squares of glass;
new-grown brick and concrete line
the flood plain, in ever relentless sheer.

The soft blue swims past in pieces,
where once it spanned the wider river
from bridge to graceful bridge.

Emptiness populates the brash towers,
dwarfing history with bland insolence.
Homelessness packs the streets
in tents of despair.

Tidal, the river rises and falls;
soft blue the pigment sky.

Flaming London

My room is hot-
spring, summer, autumn,
when is it not?

London in the inner city:
giant towers loom, more's the pity.
All that height, all that glass
mirrors down heat to we who pass;

who live in a heat sink
on the Thames flood plain.
Well, it makes you think, all the same.

How we ground dwellers,
thieved of light
lurk plaintive in the shadowed night
way down below.

The city flames with sporadic wildfire;
not yet the barbecued burning pyre,
but we're all cooking here.

British sangfroid fast declining,
still the temperature is a-climbing.
This year, next year, sometime, never:
we've lost the plot when it comes to weather.

Days

Some days pass like steam,
leave little trace but warm dampness:
droplets of love that cling to chill surfaces
like the seductive sweetness of sugar.

Other days are a miasma of melancholy:
slow days that creak along in a thick sodden trudge
through acres of claggy mud.
These are the days we blank from our memory,
shadow days eclipsed by the first full moon.

Days of the heart beating the warm rhythm of life
alternate with these painful dull days,
when we cannot bear to think.

These are the times we don't ask for help:
a message, a simple kindness,
to remind us no single person is ever alone.

Bits of Me

Bits of me are falling away
like straw from a broken nest:
floating away in the lightest gust,
the merest matter of human fluff.

Off they whisk while I am sleeping,
all the soft edges of my being;
flying like birds to far off places,
whilst I am lost in dreamy stasis.

My face is corrugated wrapping;
my inner organs awesomely lacking;
those my cells are sadly wracking.

Does this depress me? Frankly, yes.
Will it halt me? Anyone's guess.

If life were a house, I'm in the attic.
If life were a garden, I've reached the hedge.
The view from here is fine and far:
hills and dales and the morning star;
to the distant sun-lit ridge.

Gull and Chips

Waves of gulls are swooping along
the esplanade, staring down with hungry
eyes, sharp beaks poised for theft.

The beach huts line up like toy cupboards,
all bright paint and jollity. Wooden benches
high above the sands, spill over with holiday makers
all shapes and sizes, clutching packets
of freshly fried fish; vinegar-sprinkled chips
sit golden fat in their laps. The perfume of it cuts
through the seaside air with the sharpest tang.

The gulls streak across the esplanade,
dipping their wings for closer inspection.
They surf the air with Olympic grace,
wings outspread like yawns that reach
to the very tips of their feathers,
as they float cunningly nearer their goal.

The seaside diners glance up: suspicion
laces their foreheads with lines of distrust.
They know about these greedy gulls;
protectively, they hug their food tighter
in their lap, finger a mouthful with
excess caution. A single gull takes a perch
on the nearby bin. Its head swerves
longingly towards the nearby lap.

Its bony feet are creeping ever nearer; when
of a sudden, a large hairy dog bounds into view.
Wings overhead screech a warning: bin bird
stares balefully ahead. Hands are clutching fish
and chips with the passion of a nun's rosary.
The dog barks once, twice. It is close now,
very close to gull and chips.

The lone gull rises regretful in the air;
floats high above the people, up above
the toy huts, the plashing bathers.
Its eyes glare down at the peaceful scene.
It really wanted that fish, that chip.

Tomorrow is not another day. There is
only now, and more nows to come,
filled with the succulence of a beakful
of cod, one warm tender loving salted chip.

The Comfort of Chocolate
For Chantal and James

When it is all too much,
the rolling news that crushes
the crinkled leaf of hope-
comfort yourself with chocolate.

Dark and bitter, richly luscious,
a square or two and you can cope
with panic and alarm,
the hooded riders Apocalypt.

Milk chocolate bars, the palest brown,
ivory cream with fennel, our shield
against global warming: sweat drips down
the mercury climbs, what else but chocolate
in these end-of times?

Golden sea salt, New Zealand chocolate fish,
horizons may contract, but there is this:
taste transports us where we've never been-
South America, the Caribbean,
resonating flavours of the cacao bean.

History unpalatable: time for a reckoning;
justice is beckoning; the Arctic burns like glory.
There is yet sweetness in the midst of the bleakness,
dark, milk, golden and white. Take comfort in each
ruminative bite: the charismatic comfort of Chocolate.

Pigeon Pecked

He was a stout pouter pigeon
strutted along my littered pavement
with the air of royalty.

His oversized head pecked
my paper cup
with true city greed.

Finding him plain,
crude even,
I'd invested him with feathers,
jungled him in tropical primaries.

Once shat upon, twice shy.
There are too many pigeons in London
leaving white deposits
in unwelcome places.

Parallel

"Have you got a chainsaw?"

In the garden, birds swift in and out the eaves;
their wings vibrate the air as they hover a second,
scanning every which way. The trees are full in leaf
this morning in July.

Headphoned and microphoned, three young women
pour cups of steamy beverage, shoulder-length blonde
hair tied back; smocks with glaring logo, black leggings.

"What is your name? How do you spell that?"

The man at the door requests a chainsaw.
First, he'd tried the sheds. "It is the balsam," he opines,
"it spreads, takes over. Floodwater in the bottom field
drags at the toppled trees."

The house martins flicker from their nests in the eaves;
whistle through the sunlight; dart keenly from place
to place, tails forked sharp as paper.

The young women move with rapid grace;
wash and pour, splash and label: so young and already
so very diligent. Time is sweet and laced with sugar,
lattes, smoothies, cappuccinos, double expressos.

No chainsaw anywhere here, neither upstairs nor down.
"I'll try the farm the other side of the valley." Undaunted,
he strides the long grassy lane, rippling with lazy energy.

The house martins whip through the air; blinks of movement
chatter above our heads.

Lives in parallel traverse earth and sky.

The chainsaw will lop the balsam, invasive species spreading
with sure certitude among the more phlegmatic growth.
The young women dart to the counter, bright with purpose:
alive with brisk intention, cups ready for those with names.

Balsam has a stay of grace until the chainsaw cuts
its cruel way to the heart. Existence is tree to tree,
eave to evening, one paper cup and one of rounded china.

Ratty

They hunched on bar stools,
the three musketeers, sans muskets.

One cradles a Chihuahua. "Can't put 'er down,"
he says, with a proud grin. "Three years old, she be."
"Yours is she?" asks the woman opposite,
perched on her own bar stool.

These are the regulars.
Much is known and much is silence.

This is a flat land, where secrets are held close,
hugged tight as first love.
They define the contours of the land,
its reed lakes and rivers.

"Naw, ah swapped 'er fer mine from a friend,"
he smirks. No one comments. "Just fer an hour.
Goin' to Thailand soon," he observes.

"Gettin' yoursel' a bride?" queries one.
"Eh?" he shakes his ratty head, rubs his small moustache
in perplexity. "Naw, was havin' a drink wi' me mate an'
he says 'Let's go on holiday.' Next thing, it's booked,
taxis n'all."

Surprised silence. Swallows of beer. The bar person averts
her gaze, polishes a shiny glass.

"Cost 2 grand," he moans. "Cheaper to have gone
ter Yorkshire. An I hate flying."

"Take valium," says one.
"Tried it. Doan't do no good. Drinking doan't help neither."
"Wacky-bac?"

Three men sat on their stools, supping beer. 1 o'clock.
The chihuahua nestles sweetly in Ratty's lap. They lean
close and talk low, like figures in an old Dutch painting.

The wind breezes over the car park, the empty swings
the flapping awning. A lone police car moves cautiously
along a neighbouring street, seeking out its prey.

"I'm off, me," murmurs Ratty, gently placing the chihuahua
on the gravelled ground. She gazes up at him beseechingly,
paws scrabbling among the loose stones.

He bends down towards her, hands outstretched.

Manorbier

small stones pastel pink, sky blue,
the lightest banana yellow
layer the beach like pebble confetti.

a small stream swishes its frothy skirts;
skims music over smoothed stone
to the shifting sea.

far above, alone on the dim heights,
the slighted castle stands guard
over the wide car park.

paths drift down through the meadows
into another time,
when all was urgent haste
and the silvery clang of metal.

But this is now.

the empty beach counts its coloured pebbles;
water laps into the headlands,
gathers in seaweed pools where tiny creatures
live and die in the reflection of a sky;
their vast imaginings layered with striated cloud.

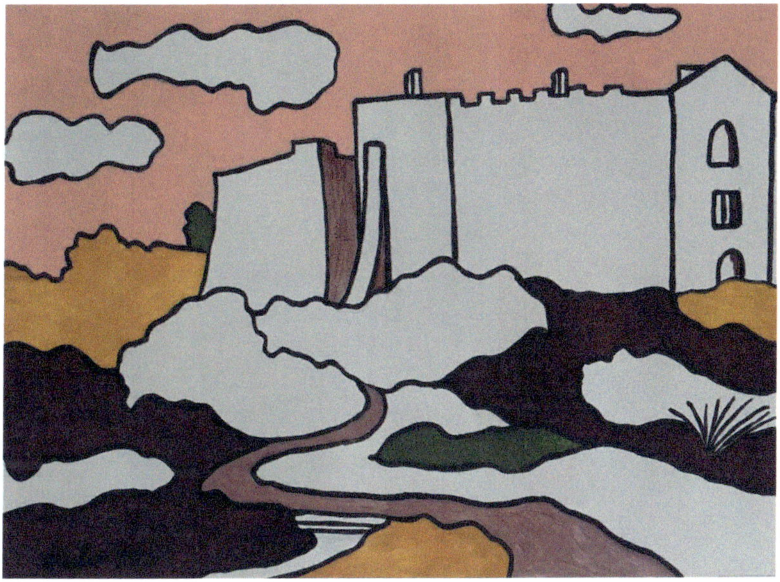

Sunburn

Sun blinded. Cool wintry sun exploded
into whiteout, stumbling along, head down,
eyes averted. Overhead, a fireball is aflame,
its dazzle aura, blue, red and gold.
I falter in the raging glare.

Nothing to see here:
Nothing but snowball radiance,
shooting stars, alarmed vision.
Cascades of light flicker like meteor tails
across eyes open and eyes closed.

Despatched to A & E purgatory
cramped waiting rooms peopled
with twitched anxiety;
old, young, seated, standing, leaning
in rumpled corridors against yoghurt-white walls.
We are listening, as the hours falter past,
for our maimed names to be called.

Godot is asleep, propped on a bench
in a patch of wandering sunlight.
Our names are stuck fast
like dead insects trapped in amber;
nothing much keeps on happening.
The future is shrouded in brume.
What you see is what you get:
which of us can see the future?

Patient Waiting

Nerves stretched thin like skipping elastic
hooked between white socked ankles:
a deft affair of cats cradle with feet for fingers,
in the playground before the whistle calls us in.

Awaiting tests, awaiting results, fearful
to grieve those I love. Willing to be free from
interventions- euphemism for spiky treatment.
I have been here before. Have you?

My eyes play tricks on me, vision flames and flickers;
kidneys weaken, spill forth froth like fast-poured beer.
My body is shrinking back to bare bone. Dread fills me.
Sleep beckons, yet when I lay down, my mind ticks over
like a backwards clock.

I need more time going forwards, then don't we all,
we who have the luxury of waiting safe in our homes
where no bombs fall, except in our fraught imagination.

It's a gamble, the surgeon said, with a rueful smile.
Wait to see where the dice fall. Alea iacta est.
So now I wait. Each day, each hour is a gift of time.
I am still afraid of the dark; but I am learning to ride
the winds of change before the whistle calls me in
from the playground, skipping ever so lightly.

Motorbike
for Rowan

Hold fast the cambered road, leaning
into the future, this now.
Corners sweep by in curves, ripple
down sandy lanes this quiet burr
wheels leaning out, tree branches
clasp one another in leaves.

Time tours byways, holding on past politics,
past covid, hands gripped gauntlet
past things stationary, a blur already past.
Leaning in, bike whips over tarmac
untrammelled, weaves past cramped
queues of cars, lorries holding the road
like pencils on paper. Sweet freedom
unlocks hidden places, Chagall flying beyond
mortality wounds, tired clocks dull with duration.

The motorbike wraps Kent, Surrey, Hants, Gloucs,
Sussex, Suffolk: skims through green overhang shade,
cloud shadowed ways, thick rain puddling down,
sheeting the visor in a watery mist.

Static, such griefs soak the news, wheel gingerly
over potholes, unfillable this age of casual untruth.
Saddled and ride the setting sun, flame gold,
my darling. Ride the failing light, dusk dark
the winding road to the lamp-lit city.

The Aquadrome   For Edith

So here we are, strolling the Aquadrome,
the three of us and baby Edith. The fifth
one, with the twisted knee sits anchored
by the lake, drawing books, pencils at bay:
paperback thriller a thin compensation
for freedom to walk unhindered.

As we perambulate the lake, pram and all,
baby Edith beams at the floating ducks.
She has big thoughtful eyes.
A direct discerning gaze,
seven months old and counting

This aquadrome is, so the signs say,
an LNR, which initials stand portentously
for Local Nature Reserve. It is not local
to us, traipsing across the metropolis.

But who is quibbling, when the 'cootchies',
the baby coots, ducks and geese stampede
towards us, beaks grunting their demands:
we are stood at the Official Feeding Station.

The swans hold themselves aloof
nested in their pristine plumage,
a considered eye to assess their chances.
There is something of Edith in their gaze,
that clear direct don't-mess-with-me stare
as they glide back into the sun-streaked water.

Edith beams at her mummy and daddy,
the source of contentment so rich
it dribbles from her lips like milk.

Edith's eyes are closing on the day.

The fifth one settles on the wooden seat;
snaps the lake, the sedge, his B6 to H6 pencils
ready to dart like damselflies over blank pages.

The sun bores down on us all, rivers of gold.

Edith is asleep.

Another Year

The most precious gift, the jewel of time,
shimmers.

So much gets fumbled, in the everyday;
slides between our fingers like worn scraps of soap.

To-do lists droop with unattended consequence:
delayed promises grouch to one another.

There is a path wavers its way into the hills,
raising dust like motes of light.

One year has passed like a flicker book,
each leaf complete in itself;
brushing past its neighbours
to riffle into a record of small moments writ large.

How many moments make a life?
Who can measure our butterfly span and pin it
to the wall of memory?

List of Illustrations

1. The Botanic Garden — Photograph JMV
2. Dark Matter — detail from painting by Rowan Vuglar
3. Slipper Socks — old family photo/source unknown
4. Deep Waters — old family photo/source unknown
5. Man Up a Ladder — screenshot /action painting video JMV
6. On The Way Back — painting by Rowan Vuglar
7. Emporium — Photograph JMV
8. Gull and Chips — Photograph JMV
9. Manorbier — Painting by Rowan Vuglar
10. The Aquadrome — Photograph JMV

BV - #0049 - 150324 - C15 - 198/129/4 - PB - 9781805141419 - Matt Lamination